Women of the Native Struggle

Women of

Edited and photographed by
Ronnie Farley

Portraits
&
Testimony
of
Native American
Women

the Native Struggle

With an introduction by
Anna Lee Walters

Herman J. Viola, Editor
The Library of The American Indian

Orion Books / New York

All of the royalties from this book go to support projects concerning Native women.

Published by Orion Books, a division of
Crown Publishers, Inc., 201 East 50th Street,
New York, New York 10022
Member of the Crown Publishing Group.
Random House, Inc. New York, Toronto, London,
Sydney, Auckland

Orion and colophon are trademarks of
Crown Publishers, Inc.

Manufactured in the United States of America

Women of the native struggle: portraits and testimony of Native American women/edited and photographed by Ronnie Farley; with an introduction by Anna Lee Walters. —1st ed. p.   cm. — (The Library of the American Indian) 1. Indians of North America—Women. 2. Indians of North America—Social condi-tions. 3. Indians of North America—Religion and mythology.   I. Farley, Ronnie. II. Series.
E98.W8W66 #1993
305.48'97—dc20   93-14975CIP

Book design by Peter A. Davis

ISBN 0-517-88113-6

10 9 8 7 6 5 4 3 2 1

First Edition

NOTE ON THE PHOTOGRAPHS
All the photographs in this book were taken with Kodak Tri-X or Plus-X film using a Nikon F3, Leica M4-2, or Hasselblad 500 C/M, and were printed by David Wong Custom Photo Lab of New York City.

for mom, dad,

alex

and

all of those whose voices have been silenced

CONTENTS

Introduction by Anna Lee Walters   9

Preface   17

REMEMBERING   **27**

LIFE GIVERS   **43**

THE LIGHT WITHIN   **59**

THE EARTH AS OUR MOTHER   **75**

THE VIEW FROM THE SHORE   **97**

THE CHILDREN: OUR FUTURE   **119**

The Women   141

Acknowledgments   149

Organizations   153

INTRODUCTION

Charmaine White Face, Ontario, Oregon, 1992

No one knows with certainty the entire population of North America in prehistoric times before the coming of the European, but a recent article reported tribal people had been on the continent for over 10,000 years. Many tribes would say that it has been much longer. The article said also that on the plains of Texas, the oldest known remains of an Indian woman had been found and her age was dated at 11,500 years. Who was she? Did she know the lineages that she would conceive? Did she know that one day she might be described as the first woman of the Native struggle?

Very little is known in modern times about the women of the indigenous population in North America that has been present for centuries, but they obviously bore considerable responsibility in the people's struggle for survival and shared in the celebration of their tribes' successful periodic adaptations to new elements in their cultures and their continuity against all odds. Though tribal women's roles have changed over time, women continue to share in the struggle of America's native peoples, and often they are at the forefront.

In the most recent US census, about one million people declared themselves to be Native American or American Indian, whatever these ambiguous terms may mean. Some groups suggest, however, that two million may be closer to the real figure. Probably more than half of this population is female, and the majority of these women will also be found to be the head of the household, in addition to being the main or sole wage earner in the nuclear family. Their economic status will be mainly low income, in the range of $12,000 to $15,000 a year, although they are also more likely to have the most formal education in the household. They will also speak English fluently and possess fragmented tribal language skills, if they are able to speak a tribal language at all. A great number of the older generation will have attended a federal government boarding school. They will have mothered at least two children and possibly as many as six. It is extremely likely that they will be grandmothers too, with at least two grandchildren, and they often provide some financial support of them.

Beyond these statistics are more important truths about the Native woman. As in days of old, to be individually self-sufficient and economically productive is still viewed as her shared responsibility. But unlike older days, the fact that nowadays she has a crucial role as a wage-earner is changing her place and her traditional role in tribal society. These kinds of external forces make new and different demands upon her that are both positive and negative. Often now, she is viewed as a "model" for younger tribal women today

simply because of her economic role and young people often equate her income alone with success, even as low as it often is.

Besides wage work, the modern Native woman must deal with encroaching urban settings, changes in family units, new health and social problems, formal education, competition in the job markets, and meeting numerous other challenges. Besides earning a living this woman also often manages the daily activities of the family. She still performs child care and care of the elderly and handicapped, in addition to running the household, which are more traditional roles. And then within a tribe, there are elders, herbalists, clan groupings, spiritual leaders, tribal-language-only

speakers, bilingual speakers, partially western educated, traditionally educated, college educated, "professional" women, and on and on, depending upon the tribal group.

Modern American society for the most part has passed through a western education system that breaks down lifestyles and life cycles of the cultures and lifestyles exposed to it into the smallest units for study and examination, habitually separating politics from social life, medicine from education, and so forth, of all cultures and lifestyles exposed to it, in much the same way academic disciplines or areas of specialization are now separated or viewed in our everyday life, and this fragmentation will prevent anyone from perceiving tribal lifestyles on this continent as they were a century or a millennium ago. In more traditional tribal lifestyles these cultural aspects have been fully integrated with each other.

Thus, in those societies, leadership involved being a statesman or woman; possessing practical and specialized knowledge about religious and philosophical matters; having concern for group welfare; being a mediator or a liaison between the people and other forces, in addition to demonstrating numerous other skills. Herbalists were mothers, religious leaders, historians, botanists, and so forth, to give an example. It was very difficult to pinpoint where one role parted from another. In some tribes today, this is still true.

Women of course have held various roles within their tribes and in some cases either determined leadership criteria or appointed leaders, in addition to serving as leaders themselves. Depending on whether or not a group was matrilineal or patrilineal, or practiced elements of both, women were very much informed and involved in the process of deliberation and selection of leaders, at different levels, in most tribes. This, too, is true today.

Each tribal group is distinguished by languages and unique teachings which it holds as evidence of its special places in the universe. Oral tradition in the forms of songs, prayers, ceremonies, and storytelling transmits language and values in much the same way these have been passed on for centuries now, although some of the information has now been translated and retold in English.

The core of teachings embraced by each tribal group accounts for the way the universe is and the place of human beings in it. In the earliest times and in still most cases yet, these were considered sacred because of the way the teachings reached the people and brought them through the centuries. Among these teachings are found descriptions of "female" beings who become the archetypes or models for modern day women of a particular group, and these are not always "human" beings. This departure from a strictly human world into something much bigger and non-human is a characteristic that marks all tribal world views on this continent, and it is a difficult concept to grasp for those outside the tribes.

Core teachings of a particular group have also always been affected by the physical environments in which the group lived. Virtually every tribe developed a unique cosmology that of course ultimately entered into women's identity, place, roles, and responsibilities. Even tribal calendars today are extensions of this knowledge and interaction with the universe, and they demonstrate careful observation of the sky and earth. Nature's laws as they were understood by each group were therefore the center of the group's core teachings.

There were also teachings which applied specifically to male and female groupings. Tribes commonly practiced naming ceremonies, puberty ceremonies, marriage ceremonies, funeral ceremonies, and memorial ceremonies. Females were taught appropriate behavior for childhood, marriage, motherhood, and old age. These teachings and ceremonies are carried on in modern life in some tribes.

In the last fifty years on this continent much technological change has occurred and tribal people here have of course been touched by it. Now, modern Native people live on reservations and in the cities. "Indian land" and "Indian country" are a very real part of American society and congressional legislation. New social programs and institutions have been introduced to the people, with varying degrees of "success." Conflict is still very much a part of the relationship between tribes and the federal government and of tribal people's interaction with larger American society. In the last 500 years, Native people have been tested on countless levels. Were it not for the efforts of both men and women in each tribal group, Native people would not be who or where they are today.

Though still a small minority in American society, collectively called American Indian or Native American, they nevertheless know who they are and what their continuing presence has meant over millennia. Tested beyond human understanding and endurance so many times since they were born here, they have consistently returned to the most ancient reference points to guide them to the present day. The miracle of their survival is not really seen and understood in that larger political and collective identity of federal government or western society, but in the survival of their diversity, those small groups (sometimes numbering a few hundred people) living and journeying successfully down through time.

The women in this book, their images and voices, tell us about what this journey has meant for them.

This book presents a selection and a point of view: these are not the only images and stories of Native women. Even within these pages is a diversity of experiences and beliefs. But there are threads that tie these women together. Change is a part of their descriptions: changes in lifestyles, changes in family units, changes in fashion, and changes in technology, to name a few. In the midst of all this, these women rely on ancient tribal teachings to guide them through and keep their eyes on the universe rather than on the behavior of erratic human beings. This is what has grounded these tribal peoples and given them survival skills to reach the present generation.

Anna Lee Walters

PREFACE

✴

I have been a photographer for as long as I can remember. Yet it has been a challenge for me to achieve recognition for my way of seeing. It is especially difficult to succeed if one doesn't want to conform, if one wants to express a personal point of view, if one has a different vision of reality. But in those brief periods when I was not consumed by merely trying to survive, I photographed the world as I saw it, a visual record of my experiences.

By 1985, I had left the work force and mainstream grind to devote myself to my photography. In my tenement building in lower Manhattan, a neighbor of mine had a brother working closely with the Diné (as the Navajo call themselves) in an area of northern Arizona called Big Mountain, where, I learned, thousands of Diné were facing forced removal from their lands, all for a national energy policy that had been developed decades before. It was a policy that entailed mining some of the richest coal and uranium fields in the world in a manner so destructive that the region had been labeled by the United States Department of Energy as a "National Sacrifice Area." Even though I was thousands of miles away, living in a world far removed from the Diné, I found myself getting involved.

My first visit to the Diné lands was in the winter of that year. I had never been to the Southwest or to an Indian reservation. The car ride to the "rez" is still etched in my mind. I saw a changing landscape of light and vibrant pastel color, with twisted, worn mountains of rock sculpted by the elements, standing alone amid vast open spaces. Suddenly I understood the word *freedom* as I never had before. It was this land that gave birth to freedom—a land undeveloped, wild, and sovereign. And in this freedom, I felt the spirit of time, a thread to the ancient past, and saw myself as small and insignificant.

As I got to know them, I found the Diné themselves were equally inspiring. Their way of life was so intertwined with the forces of their environment. Their language was unfamiliar, but their faces told the stories of working with these natural forces and of their endless struggle to maintain that way of life.

I realized that this land is here, preserved, only because someone took the responsibility of stewardship. And that is why the struggle is so important—it became clear to me the Indian wars had never ended and that the Native people continue to fight for justice and to preserve their way of life.

I also understood why Native women have a central role in this struggle. Their cycles are attuned to the natural world, they play a crucial part in the future of the people and the planet. In their traditions, a woman's life is viewed as a metaphor for Mother Earth. I was in the midst of some powerful truths.

In trips across the country over the next few years, I began to experience the tremendous strength, the vitality of culture, and the deep spiritual richness that Native people have struggled so long to maintain. At the same time I also to began understand the harsh reality of Native existence. The white world, which had already taken so much away from Indians, was still not satisfied. At every turn, Indians would be forced to conform, to yield what little they had, to be pushed off their lands if need be, to satisfy the demands of a society that was bent on consuming and relentlessly destroying every inch of this continent.

Everywhere I went it seemed that some new injustice was about to befall Indian communities: They were fighting to preserve land, to combat overdevelopment, to prevent toxic-waste dumping and the disposal of other noxious elements that no other community would accept, or they were simply fighting to worship in the manner of their ancestors. And somewhere, somehow, there would be the hand of the United States government, a trustee of Indian affairs in name only, or there would be a corporate interest—both willing partners in countless schemes to defraud Indians and taxpayers alike.

Spearheading many of the fights against these policies were the Native women. Women such as Myra Sohappy and Yet Si Blue, who continued to fish in the rivers of the Northwest as the old treaties stipulated, ignoring unjust new laws, even when they were arrested, harassed, and beaten. They would fight because they were defending their life; their life *was* the fish.

So it would be with the Western Shoshone women, Carrie and Mary Dann, who would maintain their herds of horses and cattle. Or the Diné women at Big Mountain, who would not give up their flocks of sheep to allow for coal and uranium mining. Like the Earth, they would not move.

There are also struggles within the communities themselves, where for several generations the relentless pressure to assimilate has been taking a devastating toll. There are a multitude of women within Native communities, like Roberta White Calf of the Pine Ridge Reservation and Betty Cooper from Oakland, California, who, through their work, are battling the years of Christian, corporate, and government domination whose effects are seen in alcoholism, drug abuse, domestic violence, child abuse, and suicide.

Yet amid all this, there exists a warmth and lightheartedness at the core of Indian culture—a sense of integrity, a depth of friendship, a generous hospitality, the warmth of the extended family, and a sense of connection that seems lost in the rest of America. I treasure the new friendships that have shown me the strength of endurance—endurance fueled by having something to believe in and knowing it deeply.

Whenever I would return to New York City, I would find it frustrating to approach the media with information relating to Indian struggles. Unable to break through the invisible barrier that surrounds mainstream news, I even tried working at a news service for a while, thinking it might be a way to get the issues addressed, only to be faced with a system orchestrated for the bottom line. Indian struggles are not "news," are not sensational: only when acts of violence occur do these stories get reported. I clearly understood the mechanism before me; it was the same mechanism the people on the land were fighting against, only with a different mask.

In the spring of 1988, I was approached by a member of the board of directors of the Learning Alliance, an alternative educational organization in New York City, which had been organizing forums on Native issues. They had just finished the program "Women of the Native Struggle"—which focused on the contributions of women in Native politics, the arts, medicine, and so on— and they felt I might want to turn this idea into a book.

So began a journey across America that has occupied much of the past four years. I have trekked over forty thousand miles between land and sky, from the belly of the urban beast to the back roads far away from the interstates and asphalt networks. The miles in between were spent interviewing women and photographing them in their environment, meeting families and friends, and surveying the landscape and its contrasts. I was awestruck at nature's venerable beauty and powers of revitalization, and I came to know what was and is worth fighting for. From clearcutting of the national forests of the Northwest and the ancient redwoods of Northern California, to uranium mining on Indian lands in the Southwest, to coal stripmining on Hopi and Diné lands in Arizona and on the Crow reservation in Montana, to fluoride poisoning of the waters on the Akwesasne reservation in the Northeast, to development on reservations throughout the country— despoliation of the Earth is displacing the people of the land, threatening the balance in their way of life, and endangering all of our futures.

As Kanaratitake says, the backbone of any struggle is the women—the wellspring of strength and catalysts for change in any culture. Although this book shows only a few of the many courageous and dedicated Native women working for their people, for their children, for all children, and on behalf of Mother Earth, it really is all about women and their responsibility. But it is also about a people, a particular people of the Earth, as varied in culture as the Europeans or the Africans, yet respectful of one another's diversity. And, most important, it is about a common thread in us all—our connection to the Earth.

Ronnie Farley

NOTE ON NOMENCLATURE

There is no single, agreed upon way to refer to the original inhabitants of North America. "American Indian" is incorrect, arising as it does from Columbus's geographical confusions. "Native American" is by no means universally accepted, since, properly speaking, anyone born in this country is a "native American." Also, it connotes a status akin to Italian American or Irish American, whereas many Indians do not consider themselves "American" in that sense. In general, I have used the term "Native people."

It would be more accurate to identify individuals by their particular tribes. But even here it is difficult to find the most accepted or accurate name, because often a tribe's best known or "official" title is not what the tribe calls itself, but rather the name applied to it by another people. Sometimes it is even a pejorative term: for example, the word "Sioux" is a French distortion of an Ojibway word for either "cutthroat" or "snake," depending on the translator. Furthermore, the Sioux are actually four separate peoples who share a similar language: the Lakota (Teton Sioux); the Dakota (Santee Sioux); and the Yankton and the Assiniboine (also known as the Nakota). The Lakota have seven divisions, or "council fires," of which the Oglala of Crazy Horse and Red Cloud, the Hunkpapa of Sitting Bull, and the Minneconjou, who were massacred at Wounded Knee, are the best known.

While I have tried to use the most common names and remain consistent, ultimately I have deferred to the individual preferences of the women I interviewed.

Women of the Native Struggle

REMEMBERING

Scouts, Chief Big Foot Memorial Ride, centennial of
the Massacre at Wounded Knee, Pine Ridge, S.D., 1990

When I was a child, everything was different. We didn't have highways through the reservation and we were isolated here. In the winter, it would really get bad. You could hardly get out in a car, but we traveled in wagon or on horseback when we needed to go to the store for something like flour, coffee, and sugar. We had our own food to eat, like the roots—different kinds of roots that we would dig during the spring, when they come out. That used to keep us really busy because we had to put those away, preserve them for winter. We always had a lot to eat because we had dry fish, dry meat, and other foods. Now, we don't put away as much as we used to. We always have to run to Safeway now and buy our groceries. It has changed so much since then.

Sylvia Wallulatum, Warm Springs

Sylvia Wallulatum, Warm Springs, Oregon, 1992

Yet Si Blue and Anita Paz, Yelm, Washington, 1991

We are salmon people. Everything—all our legends and thanksgiving ceremonies—centered around the salmon. When the salmon were coming upriver, we had different songs of welcoming for each one of them, giving thanks to each one for coming back again and providing us with the sustenance of life. A very elaborate ceremony took place.

There were very few things you could get punished for in our society, but the punishments were extreme. For example, nobody was allowed to go up the rivers and raise noise or be angry when the salmon were spawning, because that was a nursery. Among some tribes, if a man dared to urinate in the river, that was a death penalty. Can you believe all of our rivers are open sewers now?

**Yet Si Blue
(Janet McCloud),
Tulalip**

29

When I was eight, my grandfather told me that in order for me to survive, I had to learn the non-Indian way of living. I had to learn their language, beliefs, and their culture in order to survive.

I remember my grandfather braiding my hair. He had a leather thong that he had braided into my hair. As he spoke, he said, "With this wrap braided into your hair, you will never get lost. You will know where you came from as long as this is in your hair." And he tied a leather thong around each of my wrists and ankles and said the same thing. Then he took me up to where the residential school was and he placed me in their hands and he walked away. It was really hard to keep from crying.

They took me and the first thing they did was to pick up a great big pair of scissors, and they took my braid and they cut it. I remembered my grandfather's words and I just started screaming. I screamed and I fought, I fought and I screamed, and I wouldn't let them touch the other side [of my head]. That was my first experience with non-Natives.

**Lena Dunstan,
Malkameen,
Haida**

Delle Big Crow braiding her son Jamil's hair, Rapid City, South Dakota, 1992

Growing up in New York City, it seemed as though I was the only Indian person other than my family. All through my schooling, from elementary to college, I never met another Indian student. I still remember the sting of racism when we skimmed over the misinformation on American Indians in our history classes.

When I talk about my family, it's such an isolating experience. My home was always very separate from my outer life. I felt very guarded about my family life, and much of that stems from the fact that my mother is a seer. It was very hard growing up without the support of a larger Indian community that understood that kind of thing. Not understanding a whole lot myself about this phenomenon, I knew for sure the non-Indians I knew then understood a whole lot less. I used to be fearful of what my mother would say. It is only recently that I have begun to listen more closely to what she says and to understand that much of what goes on is not tangible. I didn't understand a lot of the things that she said because it didn't go along with what I was taught in the larger society.

**Leota Lone Dog,
Lakota,
Mohawk, Delaware**

Purepecha women, Bocaneo, Mexico, 1990

31

I joined AIM [the American Indian Movement] when I was fifteen. At that time, I was starting a relationship with my first husband. I married him when I was sixteen. In Pine Ridge at that time you had AIM on one side and GOONs [Guardians of the Oglala Nation] on the other. Most of my family were on the GOON side, so I quit high school, and wherever my husband would go, I would go with him.

When I was eighteen, my oldest daughter was born. During that time, we were really harassed by the GOONs. It was hard to live in Pine Ridge. A lot of people were dying suspiciously and getting shot, and what hurt most was that this was my reservation.

My husband was shot in Seattle. We had gone out there for the summer, and when he recovered, we came back and things didn't change very much for us. If anything, they got worse. We lived in Rapid City for a little while and we would come home to Pine Ridge, only to find our house broken into. When we would try to go back to the reservation, someone would chase us or the cops would harass us. All during this time, I was very frightened because I was so young and no one had ever prepared me to deal with being harassed by my own people.

Later, we moved back to the reservation and our second daughter was born. We had trouble and she was born early. I was in the ambulance and my mom and my husband were following behind when the cops stopped them and wouldn't let them go through. Here's my mom, the nicest person, she didn't have a gun, but they made her get out. By the time they got to the hospital, I had already had my daughter. Things like that—it was just too much for me.

After my daughter was born in October, things just went downhill. I knew something really bad was going to happen; my husband had said it would if something was not done. He went to a meeting and never made it back alive. He was killed that evening. Even after that, things didn't ease up for me at all. The people that were responsible for his death would harass me and my little kids.

I never even thought about it until maybe a couple years ago. I guess I was just protecting myself from all those thoughts and bad memories. I just had to go with what I believed in, because I don't think there was any other way I could have gone. I always think, if it was a hard time for a family, the whole tribe must have really suffered.

Delle Big Crow, Lakota

March against relocation at Big Mountain, Navajo Reservation, Arizona, 1986

Black Hills, South Dakota, 1992

Delle Big Crow at the Black Hills, South Dakota, 1992

I started being a spokesperson when I was in kindergarten. I knew what the teachers were saying. I knew what was really being said behind our backs and what we were being called. I'd always keep my ears and eyes open and I'd organize the rest of the kids: "This is what's going on, what's happening. . . ."

The one that influenced my life the most was my maternal grandmother. She was bilingual. When I think of it, what a woman she was. I took it for granted. I assumed that everybody's grandmother wrote letters to the governor, wrote letters to the editor, and spoke before groups. Incidentally, she was a Christian. She was a real strong Christian—one of those who lived by the Golden Rule, do unto others, love thy neighbor. But she was also one who didn't stand by. I asked her one time, "How come there are no Indians living in the Black Hills?" She said, "We wouldn't live there, anyway. You don't live in a church. It is sacred ground to us. But it is ours and it was taken illegally, and don't you forget that."

I didn't know that women were supposed to be the weaker sex, and I guess back in the fifties and sixties, that was the way women were supposed to be. Maybe they were in the outside world, but we sure weren't. We came from a very matriarchal family and that shaped my life.

When I'm dead and gone, I want to leave something. I want my granddaughter to be sitting someday talking like I talk about my grandmother. That's the kind of legacy I want to leave. I want my great-granddaughters, great-grandsons, too, to say, "My great-grandma was a fighter. She did this and she did that to protect the land, to protect the culture, to protect the language, to maintain what we have left."

**Madonna Thunder Hawk,
Lakota**

*Madonna Thunder Hawk, Rapid City,
South Dakota, 1992*

34

When I was a teenager, I went to Alberta to a big powwow and something happened there. I saw things that I had not seen in years. There was a medicine man there who started talking, and I was transfixed watching him because it brought back so much of my grandfather. He made me feel really good. I realized that this is what my grandfather was saying: Take from the white man what you need, but never ever forget that you are from here. I don't have to worry anymore—this is my culture right here. My grandfather said learn their language. I've done that. He said learn their skill. I have done that, too. In order for you to survive, you have to know all of those things, because they are coming by the thousands, like ants, and they are taking over. As annoying as ants are sometimes, the white man can be just as annoying. You learn how to deal with the annoyance. You do not have to get stuck and worry about getting hurt. Those were the lessons that he told me when I was going to school that first year. As I was listening to that medicine man talking, it all came back, and I said, "Yeah, this is the knowledge I have and I will no longer feel lost."

Lena Dunstan,
Malkameen,
Haida

Lena Dunstan with her granddaughter Alicia, Yelm, Washington, 1991

My grandfather was Nicholas Black Elk. I was just a little girl at the time that book [*Black Elk Speaks*, by John Neihardt] was written. My father was the interpreter. My grandfather always lived with us, and we took care of him until he died. He was ninety-seven years old.

In his own way, he was a very holy man. People were afraid of him because of that. When he talked to you, he looked like he could see right through you and he knew what kind of character you were. He would point it out.

As a little girl, I always remember him talking to us about how we should get a good education. He told us to learn what we could because someday we would compete with the white man. He told us not to forget our Indian language and our Indian culture; to learn these things and teach them to our children so it would not die out. That is what he called the Sacred Hoop, which he said had been broken. I always wondered what he meant by the Sacred Hoop being broken. I understand it now.

**Olivia Pourier,
Lakota**

Olivia Pourier, Pine Ridge Reservation, South Dakota, 1990

When I first went to school, it was hard because some of the matrons we had were really strict and mean. But as I got older, it got better. I think they taught us a lot, but they would not allow us to talk in our language. We were punished for speaking our Indian language.

Our hands were slapped with a ruler sometimes. When I went to school, I couldn't speak a word of English. I was talking in Indian and I got punished for that. On the blackboard, they'd draw three circles, and I'd have to stand up there, my face against the black-board, with my fingers on the outside circles and my nose in the center circle. I had to stand there a long time and I didn't know how to ask if I could go to the bathroom. Sometimes I'd wet the floor and I got punished all the more for that. That was the most humiliating thing that happened to me. I must have been about six.

**Sylvia Wallulatum,
Warm Springs**

Sasha Lee at home, Minneapolis, Minnesota, 1992

In our community, there were certain Indians who did certain things. For instance, if a person passed on, there wasn't a funeral director; we took care of our own. When my grandmother passed away, a man was behind our house the next morning, sawing lumber, nailing, and hammering. I went out there to watch him and he was making the coffin. There were men who did that. There were men who made ax handles for axes, men who made canes, women who made baskets. Everyone had a job, and people knew when they needed something who they could go to. The same thing with anything we did out here, there was always somebody that you could go to for different things. But it's not like that now because people don't do those things anymore. Everything is bought from the store now.

Arlene Logan,
Seneca

You have all these people bickering because they have been exposed to the education system, which teaches you that you don't need each other. So they are fighting and, of course, they want to be paid for whatever service they provide. They forget that we need one another, whether everybody likes it or not. That is what kept people together, and we don't have that anymore.

We have lost a lot of the way it was and the way it should be. There is the respect that we were always taught to have for one another. The children grew up learning respect because they lived with it. Now, I dare say it's hard to respect some people. There are things they do that turn you off and it's hard to respect them, because you see what is going on. But that respect is still there with my generation. With the younger generation that is coming up, a lot of it is missing, and they won't show it. The respect isn't there.

Maxine Parker,
Seneca

Arlene Logan and Maxine Parker,
Tonawanda Reservation, New York, 1992

I attended a mission school on the reservation and I learned a lot about brainwashing. But the most important thing I learned was the word *self-determination*, and that was something I was going to exercise. Women have self-determination, and the backbone of any struggle is the women. In our house, we were always taught what *Ganienkehaga* means—"People of the Flint." That is the true name for our nation; that is who we are.

Kanaratitake
(Loraine Canoe),
Wolf Clan,
Mohawk Nation

Kanaratitake, Brooklyn, New York, 1992

Badlands, Pine Ridge Reservation, South Dakota, 1992

LIFE GIVERS

✳

Five generations: Jenny Manybeads, Blanche Wilson, Mae
Wilson Tso, Betty Tso, and Fiona Tso, Mosquito Springs of
Big Mountain, Navajo Reservation, Arizona, 1986

Our way of life is cyclical and the first circle is the family. The heart of the Confederacy, which we call ourselves, is the family. The heart of the family is the mother, because life comes from her. The children are our essence for the future. So you see from the very beginning, the role of women is extremely important for our people.

When our circle extends, it extends to the larger family, which is the clan. The role of men is that they be fathers, uncles to all children, like women are aunts to all children, no matter what their color. When we talk about the clan, it is an extended family. Your clan is determined by your mother. Ours is a matriarchal society.

Gawanahs
(Tonya Gonnella Frichner),
Snipe Clan,
Onondaga Nation

Woman rider at Chief Big Foot Memorial Ride,
centennial of the Massacre
at Wounded Knee, South Dakota, 1990

It is really our own cultural and traditional values that we need—that has been my philosophy and my life ever since I started going to the Sundance and using the sweatlodge.

An Indian woman needs to know herself as an Indian woman first, then she can be better to people around her. If she doesn't know this, then something is always missing and something is not quite right. A lot of American Indian women suffer from low self-esteem because society has really done a number on them. I feel that when they know themselves traditionally and they know their background, their Indian identity is intact, and they are proud of who they are. And then, how do you use it? Not just one day a week; you use it in every fiber of life.

**Betty Cooper,
Blackfeet**

Betty Cooper, Oakland, California, 1991

Despite the fact that we've been struggling just to survive, we have done a very good job of preserving our traditions, because we relied on them so heavily. Women can take the credit for maintaining the different crafts, values, and making sure the children understood and participated in the different tribal ceremonies. That was our role, and we still live by that. It is our obligation to teach them these ways so that they will understand and live by them in their daily lives. The songs we sing in our sweats are so much more than just songs—our theological beliefs are in there, as well as our history and our connection to the Earth.

When the loss of culture happens, the women break down and lose that connection with the traditional value system. When they lose their connection, they begin to lose the sacredness of childbearing. Problems such as fetal alcohol syndrome have become prevalent in recent years. I believe this is one result of the alienation of Native women from their indigenous culture.

Melinda Gopher, Ojibway

Donna John, Gallup, New Mexico, 1990

Midwifery is working with the women in the most basic ways. There are a lot of women in my community I'm very proud of. I could not do what I do without having a network with other healers and other women in the community who have also worked as program directors, elected chiefs, and as counselors. Doing this work is a way of bringing the women together so that they can all witness the magic and participate in the power that birth brings to the family. I believe that our women are at their strongest when they're working together in very sacred, blessed ways.

I see changes in the women who give birth at home. They are women who are independent, who are strong, and who have strongly developed wills. I see their growth and development in carrying their birth, and then I witness them giving birth within the power of the family and not through the power of Western medicine.

Katsi Cook, Mohawk

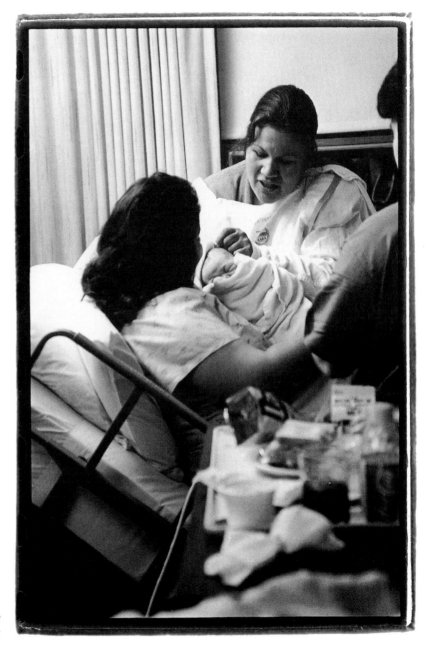

Katsi Cook with a mother and her newborn at a hospital near the Akwesasne Reservation, St. Regis, New York, 1992

A few years ago, I was having a conversation with a friend of mine at a women's conference, and I was so taken aback that women were complaining about how they just didn't want to sit at home and take care of kids. That really made me sad, because I know how important a role that is. I don't have a problem at all with that responsibility. I'm sorry if your men or other people in your lives make you feel like being a mother is something that is not worthy. I don't necessarily understand the feeling of being fulfilled as a chief executive officer, but I have an insight into it. The raising of children is looked upon as something that isn't important, yet the future depends on it and the world depends on it.

For many in our society, the role of parenting was halted by boarding schools. Our great-grandparents were prevented from being parents. Both my grandmother and my grandfather were sent away. Then their kids were brought up in a regimented, abusive system of boarding schools. What that system has done to our grandparents, our parents, and then to us and our children is put holes in the fabric of our society.

Ingrid Washinawatok-El Issa, Menominee

Ingrid Washinawatok-El Issa with her son, Maeh-Kíw
New York City, 1992

With the emergence of the feminist movement and the struggle for equal rights, people have consistently asked, "What are the Native women's issues?" People want to find a commonality with Indian people in order to understand our struggles.

In our struggle, there are not necessarily dividing lines between women's issues and men's issues. We are all struggling to survive as nations, as communities, as societies. Bringing our societies from the past, maintaining those connections into the future, and being the bridge to the next seven generations is a long upward climb. Our concern is that there be no division among the men, the women, the children, and the elders. Our society is a holistic one, and we carry with us the people, the families. Our issue is to maintain this unit and not to separate.

**Margo Thunderbird,
Shinnecock**

Lloyd and Julia John, Navajo Reservation, New Mexico, 1990

The philosophy of the Indian person in the arts is not to separate our art from our life. Our life is our art. Our art can be used for functional purposes, decorative purposes, and religious purposes.

I believe that art is for everyone. Art shouldn't be just for the museums or the rich; it should be for everyone and in everybody's home. That is why I started doing murals. That is also why I got into printmaking, because it was a way of gathering minds, a way of raising consciousness about what is happening with the Earth, Indian rights, and the Indian woman. This really goes against the whole philosophy of commercial art.

The white mainstream art world is dominated by white male aesthetics. Most of the male Indian artists have a higher position in that world because they are more accepted. But we have masters in our own art fields. Although the white mainstream tends to ignore women's art as being valid, the museums are full of baskets, weavings, and beadwork, all done by Indian women.

**Jean LaMarr,
Paiute, Pit River**

*Mae Wilson Tso cleaning wool from her sheep, Mosquito Springs
of Big Mountain, Navajo Reservation, Arizona, 1986*

We had a three-story house with a backyard in Brooklyn. I spent a lot of time in the backyard talking to myself, digging holes, and climbing fences. When I was not in the yard, looking at the sky and carrying on like that, I was in the hallway, sitting on the steps, talking to invisible people. I had a fantastic imagination, so I guess that's what helped me survive. School was deadly because we grew up in an Italian neighborhood. I was the one who was different, so they constantly made fun of me. I had been rather protected at home, living in my own little world. I did not know how to fight that, so I withdrew. I continued to withdraw from the outside world until I was an adult. When I was about ten, I started to sing. When I was thirteen, I took voice lessons and sang up until I was nineteen.

After I got married and started having children, I went back to school and studied voice and theater. I left home for Spiderwoman Theater's first rehearsal in 1975. Then our first production was in 1976. We weren't all Native then, just three of us were, and we were doing work that was avant-garde at that time. People were impressed with us because we were very controversial—all women, all ages, sizes, and backgrounds, and we were addressing issues of child abuse, domestic violence, and abuse against women.

**Gloria Miguel,
Kuna, Rappahannock**

Spiderwoman Theater Group: Gloria Miguel, Lisa Mayo, and Muriel Miguel, New York City, 1993

In 1975, Muriel asked me to join Spiderwoman Theater. It was a mixture of women with whom she worked. I hadn't been doing theater for years. I was married and was busy being a wife and a mother. I agreed and thought we would just work together for this one particular project. We would be addressing the violence in women's lives. I was a classical artist—voice and theater—so the project was very different from what I was used to.

The piece was a success on so many levels. We were able to include a lot of Native things into the piece and it opened me up to admitting who I was. I had always associated being Indian with being poor, but I had discovered so much richness in our culture. It also introduced me to the women's movement and working with women in general. It brought me back to my family, working intimately with my sisters. I began to think and grow as an artist, as a woman, as a human. I was turned on to a great freedom and power within myself. I realized I had fathoms of stories and experiences upon which to draw. I began working in improvisation and then got into writing. All of that is from Spiderwoman Theater.

Lisa Mayo,
Kuna, Rappahannock

I am the youngest one. I started as an Indian dancer. Indian dancing saved me. I spent a lot of time on the streets in Brooklyn. When it got too heavy on the streets, I retreated to my Indian friends. My friends and I were the ones who started the Little Eagles, which became the Thunderbird American Indian Dancers. Then I studied modern dance. Modern dance and Indian dancing were two different worlds.

I think it's important that people know about urban Indians. I always say "city Indian." People on reservations tend to think if you were born in the city that you don't know your culture. That is not true. People are shocked to learn that at least in New York City, we have kept the culture of our nations. When I go across this country, I know people from so many tribes. With some, I know their grandparents or their aunts or their sisters.

I am the director of Spiderwoman. I don't know if I had a vision, but I always knew I would have a group. In Spiderwoman, we can be anything we want to be. There are no limitations.

Muriel Miguel,
Kuna, Rappahannock

Spiderwoman Theater Group,
New York City 1993

53

As women, we do a lot of weaving and are gifted toward the arts. We weave so our children can eat and be clothed. Our thoughts are woven into words, as we speak and talk. Quilts are woven for the warmth of words. We weave our feelings into camera work, art, love, writing, and just being.

As I paint, I try to capture the textures of life and to show visually what we indigenous people face as a struggling nation. My paintings are quite simple on the surface, but under the colors, my heart and mind cry with pain. This is how I communicate; my art is my tool of speaking.

**Judy K. Buffalo,
Winnebago**

Judy K. Buffalo, Portland, Oregon, 1991

Seneca sisters: Janet Hill, Janis Hallett, and Maxine Parker,
Tonawanda Reservation, New York, 1992

Diné sisters: Julia John and Nellie Daniels, Navajo Reservation, New Mexico, 1990

Two Spirit people have always been a part of the tribal culture. In recovering our histories, we find that Two Spirit people were respected and held honorable positions in some of our communities. This acceptance and respect in our cultures of one's gender and sexuality is a tradition that has been lost with the advent of colonization and Christianity. WeWah and BarChee-Ampe is an organization named after two ancestors in Native American history: WeWah, a Zuni Ihamana who lived his life in the role of a woman, and BarCheeAmpe, a Crow woman warrior and leader who eventually married four wives.

A gathering of Two Spirit people was held in Minneapolis in 1988. This was an historic event, and for many of us who attended, it was the first time to be surrounded by other Indian Two Spirits. The gathering meant validation and coming out of isolation. It set into motion the creation of local organizations and networking on a national level.

It is very hard to separate struggles. My roles as a Native woman, lesbian, mother, and artist are equally important. Though I have been out for many years, I still fear rejection among Indian people because of homophobia. Acceptance of all of who I am is necessary. In our struggles as Indian people, I try to remember that part of our survival depends on understanding one another.

**Leota Lone Dog,
Lakota,
Mohawk, Delaware**

*Leota Lone Dog, Washington Square Park,
New York City, 1993*

THE LIGHT WITHIN

✳

Monty Clifford, Pine Ridge Reservation, South Dakota, 1990

In chemistry, they teach you about the atom and all of the smaller particles. Today, scientists are finding out there are smaller and smaller particles within the atom. They want to know what is the energy that pushes that electron around the nucleus of the atom. The Lakota have a very ancient belief called "the movement behind the movement" or "the motion behind the motion." That is the sacred name for God.

When, as we are taught, you can understand that God exists in everything, then you can understand the relationships between not just living things but also the so-called inanimate things, like rocks and stones. That is what balance is.

One of our old, old holy men said, "Every step you take on Earth should be a prayer. The power of a pure and good soul is in every person's heart and will grow as a seed as you walk in a sacred manner. And if every step you take is a prayer, then you will always be walking in a sacred manner."

**Charmaine White Face,
Oglala Lakota**

Charmaine White Face, Ontario, Oregon, 1992

So much of the time people look at life from a negative aspect. Something goes wrong and they say, "Everything is bad for me." But that is not the case. Navajo people believe that those are the emotions and feelings that you have in order to see how to take care of that problem. Negative feelings, attitudes, words, personalities, and conduct are not ways of sustaining yourself. Trying to control things on your own without the spiritual attachment does not take you anywhere. Understanding why certain things happen gives you wisdom and the knowledge of how to transmit that philosophy to the next generation.

By understanding those things, I believe you develop that strength within yourself that helps you know your role and your destiny in life and how you can be effective in your environment. That is empowerment. Each one of us has that ability. We are born with it.

**Esther Yazzie,
Diné**

Esther Yazzie, New York City, 1987

I have been reflecting on the past eighteen years that I have been involved with AIM. I needed a lot of strength along the way because I faced a lot of obstacles as a woman and as a Native person. The one thing that helped me through all this turmoil was the spiritual strength, the teachings and the recognition that I received from the elders.

When I was faced with a prison sentence, for example, I was terrified. There was nowhere to turn. I was facing a white court system and the prospect of going to prison and leaving my family and children. But I drew on the traditions, the culture, and the spiritual teachings. I went within. What each woman has to do is go within, find who she is, and cherish and hang on to that, because that is life itself.

Once you have that strength, that feeling of belonging and that pride, you can face anything. There is never any end to the learning. It becomes a driving force within to keep searching, and then the doors are always being opened. It is a beautiful experience. Daily prayer, no matter how brief, is the strength that keeps us going. Ask the ancestors, especially the grandmothers. They are waiting and wanting to help you.

Yvonne Swan,
Sinixt, Arrow Lakes Nation

Yvonne Swan, San Francisco, 1991

When I performed the sacred dance of thanksgiving, I wanted to know what Red Cloud had prayed for. His prayers were for seven generations of our people to live. I wanted to see my grandchildren, my great-grandchildren, and their children live. I wanted them to see a better life than the one I had seen. I did not want our children suffering all the pain that our Native people have suffered. So I dedicated myself and kept searching for the truth. It was very hard for me because I had to look within, where the truth had been all along.

There is a little spark in an Indian we call *Petaga*. He comes from the direction of the west. That spark is the light within every one of us. If we nourish that spark, and go through the healing, then the light is able to grow. Growth and change is a lifetime process.

In our Creation stories, we are given a gift by the rock spirits. They were created on the second day and they had seen the rest of Creation. They left us a gift, and that was our conscience and our common sense.

Spirituality is not something you can learn in books. It has to come from within. It is very hard, but it is also very simple. Trust in yourself; follow your conscience; go to the place inside. That is where your answers are.

**Roberta White Calf,
Oglala Lakota**

Roberta White Calf with Rocky, Pine Ridge Reservation, South Dakota, 1992

Understanding and respecting yourself is what people should strive for. The traditional people do that through the pipe and through our ceremonies. You clear your mind and your body of the negative things. It is purification. If something is on your mind and is bothering you, you pray about it, you release it, and it is off your mind, allowing you to continue your life in a positive manner. The only person who can help you is yourself. You can pray. Every spring I go to *hanblecha* [a vision quest] up on a hill and I look forward to that. Every year, whenever I go up, I get to be all alone. It's just me and God up there, to share my thoughts, feelings, hopes, dreams, and, most of all, thanks for giving me life.

**Wanbli Yaha Win
(Karen White Eyes),
Lakota**

*Wanbli Yaha Win,
Pine Ridge Reservation, South Dakota, 1990*

Mary Jane Wilson, Gallisteo, New Mexico, 1991

Indians have to pray. A lot of Indians are turning into alcoholics and drug addicts. They may think this is beautiful, but they should wake up. We have to wake up our teenagers and we are not doing it. A lot of them need help. This is why we need the salmon. We need the water to be pure, because our Creator and our ancestors say Indians are the Earth Keepers of this country. Say your prayers and balance north, south, east, and west.

**Myra Sohappy,
Columbia River**

People want to learn about spirituality so badly that they will follow anything that comes before them, but actually what they are doing is hurting themselves if they don't understand it. You have to be sincere whenever you're practicing the Indian religion; it's too sacred a thing to mess around with.

People should go right down to their own roots and learn from there, learn from their own beginnings, and then get to where they have it within themselves.

**Olivia Pourier,
Lakota**

Myra and David Sohappy, New York City, 1989

We do not separate our spirituality from reality; they are the same. Our medicine people and our spiritual people can talk to spirits; that is their purpose. In our Lakota beliefs and ways, medicine people are chosen by the spirits. I can't just say, "I'm going to be a medicine woman." I would have to have been chosen at birth. Different signs would be shown to the elderly and to the people as to who would be a medicine person, or even a teacher.

A Lakota medicine woman cannot begin to practice until after she has passed into menopause, because prior to this she will have children and grandchildren to tend to. So by the time she is very elderly, she will have the wisdom and the dedication she needs to be able to help the people.

**Charmaine White Face,
Oglala Lakota**

*Blanche Wilson, Mosquito Springs of Big Mountain,
Navajo Reservation, Arizona, 1986*

The difference between Native women and white feminists is that the feminists talk about their rights and we talk about our responsibilities. There is a profound difference. Our responsibility is to take care of our natural place in the world.

The difference between Native people and New Age people is that New Age people want spiritual experience in the same way that Americans want to go out and buy something. It is a part of their culture of wanting things without the responsibility.

They have been ripped off from their own source. They don't know who their people are; they don't know their history. Chances are that if they went back a few generations into their own history, they would find similar ways of looking at the world. My understanding is, at one point, Mother Earth religions were all over the world. In fact, that was probably the original instructions of all people everywhere. This male dominance, this white male dominance of the world, is a dangerous aberration from the natural, original instructions.

**Renee Senogles,
Red Lake Chippewa**

Renee Senogles, Bemidji, Minnesota, 1992

Casino sign in Nevada and motel sign in Texas, 1992

Our culture, our spiritual ways are being prostituted. We have pimps who call themselves medicine men, who are pimping off of our culture and our spirituality. Every now and then, my husband sits there and shakes his head. His father was a medicine man, and he was one in the days when it wasn't acceptable. Even the Indians in his own community called them devil worshipers, and put them down.

**Madonna Thunder Hawk,
Lakota**

You never mess with things of the spirit. I really believe that when you are tapping into spiritual sources, there are sources we cannot control, nor should we try to control them. We may have a relationship with them, we may benefit from them somehow, but we never control them. You are taking a risk when you abuse spiritual sources—you don't know what the results are going to be. It is just like when you abuse the natural world. You may not see that result immediately, but at some point in time there will be a result.

One of the things I respect so much about what I know of the Indian nations in this hemisphere is that there was reciprocal respect of other people's ways. There wasn't a need for one people to claim and take another people's religious belief systems or heritage. There was an understanding that this is what was given for you and that you had your way to relate to the Earth and the spiritual world, and they had their way. You didn't take their way or force your own way on them. I think that is the greatest example of how to live in a multicultural world.

Donna Chavis, Lumbee

Nevada, 1992

I never understand why some people think it's so wonderful to be an Indian. I think it is real hard, and every Indian I have ever spoken to feels the same way. We are the only group that has to prove who we are. We have all these people who want to be us. We just can't figure out why.

**Rosemary Richmond,
Mohawk**

People think they can buy religion or spirituality in a supermarket or in a drugstore, like a pill. And what can you do with people like that? If there's a market for it, there's always going to be somebody to sell it. First they were following all the Eastern gurus, and that was a big joke. Every taxicab driver from India could come over here and become a swami. Teach a few things and get a following. Maybe it's the educational system that still teaches too much "Simon Says." I know people are starved for meaning, purpose, and value in their lives because they haven't been taught at an early age that life is a gift. It's something to be treasured and used every minute, because you can't bring it back. It's a one-way road.

**Yet Si Blue
(Janet McCloud),
Tulalip**

Many are attracted to our spiritual beliefs out of a sense of curiosity or because they are searching for answers. Trying to obtain truth and understanding is a prayer. Each one of us has a gift, an ability, a purpose for being here on Earth. You as an individual know what you are supposed to do and what your abilities are. It is all very simple. It is something that exists within you.

**Charmaine White Face,
Oglala Lakota**

Pine Ridge Reservation, South Dakota, 1992

THE EARTH AS OUR MOTHER

✳

Northern California, 1992

Northern California, 1992

My grandmother used to preach about respecting this Mother Earth, which is most important in our culture, traditions, and religion. That is what everybody's problem is. They keep trying to develop this land. Why can't they have respect for her and not destroy her?

In our religion, we look at this planet as a woman. She is the most important female to us because she keeps us alive. We are nursing off of her.

The woman's body is an instrument for creating. To alter your body by using chemicals, then to carry an unborn while using these chemicals is not traditional at all. We were taught to respect our bodies as well as Mother Earth.

**Mary Gopher,
Ojibway**

Indigenous women, they're supposed to look at themselves as the Earth. That is the way we were brought up. This is what I try to tell the young people, especially young girls.

In the Western Shoshone way a long time ago, when your mother got old, you didn't throw her away; you brought her into your home and took care of her. This is the way we are supposed to take care of the Earth, too. The same way we would take care of our mothers. It's basically just common sense.

**Carrie Dann,
Western Shoshone**

Melinda and Mary Gopher, Great Falls, Montana, 1991

77

We are a matriarchal society. Even our language honors the women. It is a female language. When we dance, the men dance on the outside of the circle. The inside of the circle is to honor the women. When you dance to the ceremonial sounds of the Earth you are tickling Mother Earth and giving her joy for all the things she gives us to stay alive. When a tree moves and it gives you oxygen, you breathe. Without water, we wouldn't be alive. We come from water; we live with water; our bodies are water. You can't buy that kind of spirituality—it comes from inside; it comes from the Earth itself.

**Kanaratitake
(Loraine Canoe),
Wolf Clan,
Mohawk Nation**

Douglas fir trees, Washington State, 1992

The corn's gestational growth is very similar to the human, so corn was a very big part of pregnancy and childbirth. We knew all the medicines that came from corn. The child was blessed with corn powder.

There is a type of corn that has the kernels covering the tip, a short-eared corn, and the center kernel is used as a medicine for the baby if the mother dies. This must have been from the old days, when there was probably a higher rate of maternal mortality. They grind up one kernel, mix it with water, and give it to the baby to remind the baby it still has a mother. In the Indian world, you are never an orphan. You always have your mother the Earth, your grandmother the Moon, and all your relations in the community. So it helps. It doesn't make up for it, but it helps.

**Katsi Cook,
Mohawk**

*Dreamsong with Virgil Sohm,
Flagstaff, Arizona, 1986*

The Earth is my home.
The Earth shelters all the animals.
The Earth takes care of us.
The Earth feeds us and heals us.
The Earth watches us at night.
I love the Earth.

**Dreamsong,
Cree,
age eleven**

*Pine Ridge Reservation,
South Dakota, 1990*

Mother Earth, Oregon, 1992

Father Sky, Texas, 1992

When they reach the Moon and mess with it and bring anything back, all the female species from animal, bird, plant, and human are going to instinctively feel that in their wombs. They're going to feel the threat to life and they're going to rise from all over the world. But a lot of women are not really going to know; they are still going to fight within the cover of things like the Equal Rights Amendment. They are not going to see that women have superior rights under the Creator.

It is going to be the job of Native women to begin teaching other women what their roles are. Women have to turn life around, because if they don't, all of future life is threatened and endangered. I don't care what kind of women they are, they are going to have to worry more about the changes that are taking place on this Mother Earth that will affect us all.

**Yet Si Blue
(Janet McCloud),
Tulalip**

Full moon, northwest Wyoming, 1992

Navajo people believe that we are here today because the Creator made us. That is why everything that you are—each strand of hair, how you sit, how you talk and pronounce your words—is so important, because that is you. You are here just like the blade of grass that has every right to blow in the breeze. That is how we are tied to nature.

**Esther Yazzie,
Diné
(Navajo)**

*Kee Manybeads, Mosquito Springs of Big Mountain,
Navajo Reservation, Arizona, 1986*

This is home. This is the land here. As a mother, it is important for me to have my children here. Even though I know that in the modern world they are going to have to deal with a lot of things outside of this land, they are going to know their center. They have roots and hopefully they will have wings to go along with those roots. Even the seven-year-old is very aware of her roots, who she is and where she is. I think that is important. No matter where they are, if they can't get back to this place when they need to, their mind will bring them here. I'm sad for people who can't experience that. Not just own a piece of land with a house on it, but the whole connection—the community, the history, the stories.

Now I have enough age on me to really know the stories of the ancestors here in this land, and so many pieces of it have the story of someone. I'm related to everybody here, in some way or the other.

I feel on a very deep level that part of our separation from one another on this globe, in terms of war and so forth, is connected to people's separation from the land and the natural world in general. We've all had that taken from us in a variety of ways, but so many people are literally separated from the sense of space that their only concept of it is the ownership of it all.

**Donna Chavis,
Lumbee**

*Donna Chavis
with her daughters Rhiannon and Amanda,
Pembroke, North Carolina, 1992*

Where I live, is where my prayers are.
Where I live, is my birth placed.
Where I live, is where the afterbirths are all placed.
Where I live, the land knows me, just as I know
    the land.
On the New Lands they would not know me.

**Mae Wilson Tso,
Diné**

Mae Wilson Tso with her sheep, 1986

Mae Wilson Tso hanging wool from her sheep,
Mosquito Springs of Big Mountain, Navajo Reservation,
Arizona, 1986

People complained of all this rain—and it was miserable weather all spring and all summer—but we had the largest cabbage that we've had in years. It was so big that it fit in the bottom of a bushel basket. We also had tons of raspberries, and that was thanks to the rain.

But Norton's garden, for some reason, is always blessed. I always feel it's because we share what God gives us. That is the way you're supposed to do it, and not think, Oh, we could make money off this garden. First you provide for your family, then you provide for your relatives and your friends, and then if there's something left, there are people that may want to buy raspberries. We have just always been blessed with much more than enough for us.

Even when my kids were little, I'd have them all up in bed and I'd be down here, by myself, canning until one, two, three in the morning. I'm still doing that. It's not easy. It's hard work, but you have to want to do it. There has to be a reason and our reason is that we hope someday our children will be able to survive if the day ever comes when they do not have a job. The most important thing is to eat and to keep yourself warm, that's it.

If everyone did something for somebody else, there wouldn't be anyone in need in the whole world. Just help somebody. It's not that way now, but I think people are going to learn.

**Marlene Rickard,
Tuscarora**

*Marlene Rickard carving moose meat,
Tuscarora Reservation, New York, 1992*

We will have a ceremony to give thanks to the strawberries and we give thanks for string beans. We give thanks for a lot of things through the years. Somebody will come along and say, "When are you going to have your strawberry dance? What is the date?" We never do things by date. We don't have that form of calendar. We did it when it was ready to be done. We did it when they were ready, when they were ripe, when the things were ready to be picked. It was done when the Creator set it down. There is a time for everything.

**Arlene Logan,
Seneca**

Rams, Black Hills, South Dakota, 1992

Non-Native people have a tendency to want to fix everything. Sometimes things don't need to be fixed immediately. If you let nature take care of itself and heal itself, you will notice that it will do just that. Yellow-stone Park is a good example. It experienced charring and burning, and within less than a year's time, people began to see regrowth and the news media was shocked. Nature does this all the time. We as human beings are part of the Earth and a part of nature. Allow nature to heal and it will happen.

Gawanahs
(Tonya Gonnella Frichner),
Snipe Clan,
Onondaga Nation

Gawanahs, New Jersey, 1993

91

Mount Shasta, Northern California, 1992

Washington State, 1992

Logging truck, Oregon, 1992

What we are fighting is the development. What we are fighting is the greed, corruption, and murder—for things that should be shared. We know the enemy. We know exactly who they are. We know the companies that are tearing down the rain forests. We know the companies that are trying to tear down Big Mountain. We are all people of the Earth, the Mother Earth. That includes animals, and they need as much protection as we do.

Pat Bellanger, Ojibway

Clearcutting, Oregon, 1992

THE VIEW FROM THE SHORE

"White man's gods," New Mexico, 1989

We recognize our relationship to the past and to our future because they are the same thing. This is a cyclic way of viewing things. We also believe, in our community and in other places, that you never take more than you need. You take what you need, you give thanks for that, and you leave the rest.

When you live in a society that continues to have little regard for nature, continues to put man above nature, and continues to have laws that say that natural things do not have rights unless they are domesticated by man, you get into the desperate position we are in today.

Our view is very different from what has become the industrial or North American world view. The optimum person in this linear world view is a North American white man. He is an "advanced man" who is "civilized," and who has technology at his fingertips and economic growth in his pocket. Of course, the rest of us are left out of that process.

This is not just an isolated Indian problem; this is a problem that is based on the way the United States has chosen to live. America is a country that was founded on and continues to be rooted in a frontier mentality. "The West" is a state of mind— a belief that you can continue to move forward and that there will always be a new frontier to go to. This is a very American belief, and one that has become entrenched in our economics, politics, education, and in every aspect of every institution in the United States today. That viewpoint and that way of teaching people has had very serious implications for our nations and for our communities, and it is incumbent on us, while we struggle, to learn to change each aspect of every institution. It is a big task, but is, nonetheless, the only task that I see, because

we are dealing with systemic problems that need systemic change. We must learn to live in a society that is based not on conquest but on survival. This is not just an Indian issue; it is an issue that relates to all of us.

**Winona LaDuke,
Mississippi Band Anishinabe**

*Winona LaDuke and her son, Aajuawak Kapashesit,
White Earth Reservation, Minnesota, 1992*

Roadside attraction, Arizona, 1990

The first attack was on our food—the buffalo, the natural resource of our survival. The second attack was on our religion. If you can get at people and change their minds and souls, it's a stronger way. Economics and displacement are other attacks against indigenous people all over the world. Most of us know some of our roots. But what happens in removing indigenous people from one place to another is that you uproot a whole culture.

**Sandy Johnson Osawa,
Makah**

We have the same problems that everybody else has—drugs, alcohol, domestic violence, to name a few—and now we must address the horror of AIDS. Believing that AIDS will not attack our communities is to live under an illusion. Our immune systems have been under constant attack for the last five hundred years. This disease could drastically reduce our populations and has thus far killed over four hundred Indian people. For our communities, that is enormous. This should be reason enough for our people to wake up and address the problems. When I work in different communities or am asked to speak, I try to address the reality, whatever plane it's on. I don't want to live under an illusion.

**Leota Lone Dog,
Lakota,
Mohawk, Delaware**

Entrance to mass grave at Wounded Knee, South Dakota, 1992

100

I want to thank all of you who are concerned about my son Leonard Peltier. He isn't wasting away in prison. He is getting stronger. Leonard has more wisdom, I think, than all of us that are outside, free, and I'm really dependent on him even though he's locked up. I hope you will pray that Leonard will be free. Someday my son will be out of that prison, I know, because he's innocent, and I'm praying for him every chance I get.

When he lost his dad, he felt bad because he wasn't at the funeral. I told him it was okay if he wasn't there. "He's been with you right along. There's only one road we'll all take, so someday we'll all meet together." I told him, "I don't want you to worry, but you have to be strong and always pray."

All of our ancestors, who have died and gone ahead of us, are in paradise. The Indians call this paradise the "Happy Hunting Grounds." And they are helping us, so maybe we will get to keep our lands and our Black Hills. My great-grandfather said that the Black Hills was a suitcase that our children will eat from. That is why we don't want to sell it—we want to hang on to it no matter what.

**Hazel Little Hawk,
Lakota**

*Hazel Little Hawk, Pine Ridge,
South Dakota, 1992*

101

Hazel Little Hawk, Pine Ridge, South Dakota, 1992

Our people get tromped on, stepped on, and lied to—the whole works—but you can't dwell on pain. That is the past. With all of us working for a better tomorrow, things can get better. If we dwell on all the hurts, nothing will come from it except hard feelings. We have enough of those.

We have to work for a better tomorrow and for all the pain to heal in our spirits. Whenever something painful comes about, I believe in the Creator. He helps me to get over what is bothering me. He helps me to get over the hurt.

**Mildred Kalama Ikebe,
Nisqually, Puyallup,
Native Hawaiian**

Mildred Kalama Ikebe, Yelm, Washington, 1991

At the initial point of contact, we were on the eastern shore of North America. Since then, there has been a great decimation of our numbers, language, and culture. In the average American citizen's mind, there is no Indian existence on the eastern shore any longer, which is sad, because once people get out and find the reality of our existence and see that it is there, they are amazed at the durability, survivability, and sustainability of people who have been able to continue after so many hundreds of years and after so many attempts at devastation. They are amazed at the adaptation that has occurred under all those conditions, even to the point of our being written out of history. It is really a great statement to the spirit of the people that we have been able to survive all that time.

**Donna Chavis,
Lumbee**

Steelworker on lunch break, New York City, 1989

The Bureau of Land Management claims they own Western Shoshone land, though that is simply another way of saying they want to steal it. For years they have tried to stop us from grazing our cattle, because they claim that we are trespassers and we don't have a permit to graze on BLM property. But of course it isn't BLM property; it's Western Shoshone. Lately they have tried to round up our cattle and horses and impound them and sell them.

In September 1992 the office staff down there noticed a lot of cops running around in Crescent Valley, more than usual. It was very suspicious. So we took off through the back road. As we were coming over the hill, we met this whole caravan of people. I spoke to the man in the lead, a special BLM agent in charge, and I asked him where they were going. He said they were going to go get cattle. I asked him if they were mine. He said they were just going to get cattle that were trespassing. I started arguing with the BLM agent, and I was getting mad, and the madder I get, the better things go, I guess. I told them that I wasn't going to allow them to take my cows. I was determined that the cows weren't going to go. And I told April, one of the volunteers, "Well, us women first. If I get arrested, you jump in. . . ."

**Carrie Dann,
Western Shoshone**

Mary and Carrie Dann, Crescent Valley, Nevada, 1992

One of the things that needs to be said is that Custer was really a criminal. He was violating the treaty of 1868, and yet this man is honored. During the 1870s, this country found itself in a dilemma. The country was coming out of a recession and gold was found in the Black Hills. The government really wanted and needed that gold, but there was a peace treaty standing in the way that guaranteed the tribes of the plains their right to hunt on these lands forever.

So what were they to do? They either had to honor this treaty and respect the law or figure out a way to create a war so those lands could be won militarily. Custer was then sent on land that was to be protected by the United States government forever.

He was sent to instigate and promote a war. It was a war by provocation. This is another piece of history that is seldom told.

**Sandy Johnson Osawa,
Makah**

*Sandy Johnson Osawa,
Seattle, Washington, 1992*

The colonialism in North America, as well as in Central and South America, has been particularly brutal. Historically, it should be characterized as genocide, but we never talk about a North American holocaust. What we talk about are isolated massacres that occurred and Indian people who generally dissipated during the period of Manifest Destiny. It is very sad because, from the standpoint of knowing your history and knowing what the implications of a history are, it is very difficult, as Native or non-Native people, to piece back together what was truth.

**Winona LaDuke,
Mississippi Band Anishinabe**

*Sign marking the site of the 1890 Massacre at Wounded Knee,
Pine Ridge Reservation, South Dakota, 1990*

Road signs, 1992

We have the tendency to stereotype the Indian male and put him on a horse in the warrior syndrome. As an art instructor, I talk to my students about not creating "The End of the Trail" art because that feeds into a philosophy that was created by non-Indian people. It was a stereotype portraying Indian people as a vanishing race. So I encourage them to create art from their own background and culture and not to perpetuate the stereotype of Indian people.

Jean LaMarr,
Paiute, Pit River

Gas station, New Mexico, 1990

Road signs, 1992

You see the dichotomy that exists as to who has the power in this country in terms of shaping images. Certainly the power does not rest with Native American people in shaping their own images. It rests with the outside powers.

In the media and in documentaries, our image continues to be full of problems. The challenge is to try to understand the point of view when you see a movie or read a book. What point of view does the writer or filmmaker have?

We have been struggling for a voice to say something about the world as we see it— either through paintings, pictures, words, music, lectures, or film and video. It is a constant struggle because we do want to talk and be a part of that whole panoramic view. We feel we have something to say.

**Sandy Johnson Osawa,
Makah**

Restaurant, Colorado, 1991

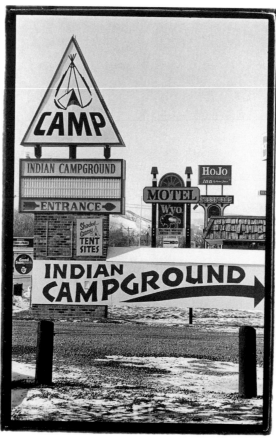

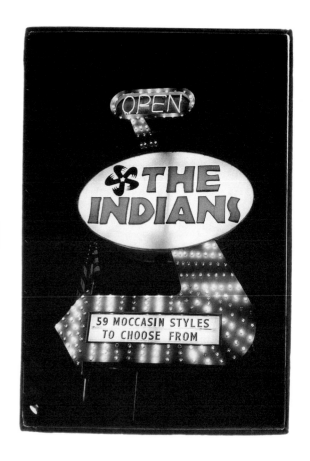

Road signs, 1992

Of all of the urban Indian centers in the country, I think the most difficult problems are here in New York City. Not because the problems are any different but because they are compounded by the size of the city and the fact that there is no Indian neighborhood in New York. Indians become almost invisible in this city.

Indians here look like anyone else, and most people don't realize that. Many people think Indians should look like something they see in books or on TV—that we grow feathers out of our heads. I'm not exaggerating. Many otherwise intelligent people really think that there are no living Indians, that there couldn't possibly be Indians in New York City, and that the only true Indian culture rests in museums.

The other problem is that of all the different cultures in this particular city, we are the smallest. So it's hard to have any political clout. We are starting to make inroads there and we have to make the city government understand that it doesn't matter that we are the smallest in number. The fact is that we have needs and we have a certain right, a unique right, that needs to be considered.

**Rosemary Richmond,
Mohawk**

*Rosemary Richmond,
New York City, 1992*

113

The corporations are going to take the place of the churches of medieval times. The churches were the powerful ones; now it is the corporations. There has always been this idea that Indians are primitive, superstitious people who don't believe in science and live in myth. But it is exactly the reverse. It is actually the Native people who live in reality, who understand the world very well; it is the Western world, the European model, that has its tremendous myths—the myth of Columbus, the myth of the United States, democracy, and the American Dream. In fact, people live in a drugged environment, a real drugged environment of illusion, TV, alcohol, and drugs. They live in a dream-world and nothing will wake them up, not even the fact that the world is environmentally coming apart, to the point where you might see a lot of people die. And the Native people are the ones who are saying, Hey, the world's coming apart! Can't you see? Can't you see what's happening?

It gets really bad sometimes. When I get carried away, I look at everything and I get so mad I could scream. I told my sister Mary, someday I'm just going to go out and cry someplace.

**Carrie Dann,
Western Shoshone**

Along the interstate, Idaho, 1992

Mainstream society has become very disposable— disposable lives, disposable relationships, disposable everything. If you don't like it, live somewhere else. I believe it's going to be harder before it's going to get better. But I sincerely hope that there is a lot of focus and direction on stopping production of things that are destructive of life. Nobody has to be a nuclear physicist to understand that if their own scientists are saying there's no safe way to store this, maybe we shouldn't be making it by the tons and tons that we are. People have this thing that if they don't see the chemicals that are being produced, then they don't exist.

Nilak Butler,
Inuit

Nilak Butler, San Francisco, 1992

Too often, Indians are divided because of other people's ideologies and their viewpoints. It is a result of colonialism. When outsiders rush in to provide their expertise and to take over our struggle, we end up fighting one another. The same ideas of Western superiority, in politics and religion, that are evidenced in the papal bulls of the fifteenth and sixteenth centuries can be found in those who attempt to help us today.

For example, how can you "Save the Earth" if you have no spiritual relationship with the Earth? There is an intellectual abstraction about the environment but no visceral participation with the Earth. Non-Indians can't change the current course of destruction without this connection; they can't see that their world is coming to an end. We are on the edge of the world and Indians know that. When you have lived on the verge of extinction, you recognize it.

**Gawanahs
(Tonya Gonnella Frichner),
Snipe Clan,
Onondaga Nation**

Margo Thunderbird, Oregon coast, 1992

THE CHILDREN: OUR FUTURE

✸

Katsi Cook with her twin sons,
Philip and Thomas, Ithaca, New York, 1992

People say it's a miracle, and it really is. I just get so excited about every birth. The Creator really did put everything here for us, and I'm in awe every time. In our culture, those children, you greet them—you are very happy to see them. It doesn't matter whether they have a father or not. I was taught that you should be happy for that child to be born, because that was our future. That person could bring peace on Earth or something even better. You never knew what the Creator had in store for that child, so you were always grateful to have that child on this Earth. That is really how it is.

Maxine Parker, Seneca

Winter Buffalo Girl Simmons and Brother Sun, West Pasadena, California, 1991

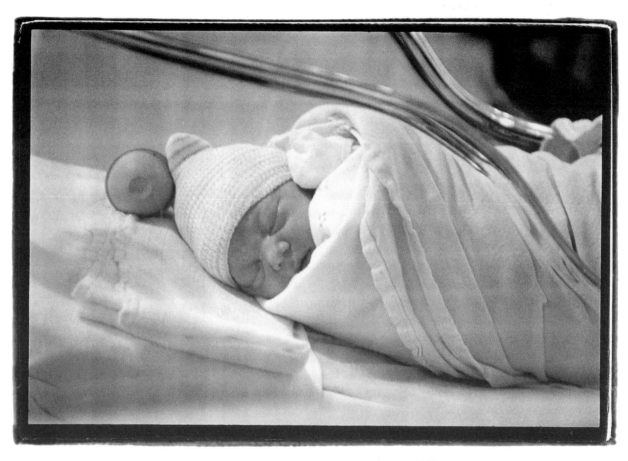

Half-hour-old Mohawk baby, northern New York State, 1992

*Waseyabin Kapashesit, White Earth Reservation,
Minnesota, 1992*

122

They say that it will be 250,000 years before the high-level radioactive waste is safe. In looking at numbers like that, it goes beyond what I can relate to in any way, shape, or form. I had to translate it into something that I could understand. So I did it by generations—approximately twenty years per generation. That's 12,500. Twelve thousand five hundred generations are going to have to deal with the garbage produced in these times. What a legacy.

**Nilak Butler,
Inuit**

Pat Bellanger with grandson, Minneapolis, Minnesota, 1992

I get afraid at what I see happening in the world. I get real afraid for the future of children. You can't just teach kids to say no to drugs. You have to give them that strength and spiritual empowerment so that they can resist the negatives. You have to give them something that will help them feel good about life.

**Yet Si Blue
(Janet McCloud),
Tulalip**

The twins, Ithaca, New York, 1992

We want our children to live in peace. As adults, we literally have to show the young people there is a way. We have to show them not to be abusive and that there is a way to undo the abuse that we have already suffered. Abuse can be carried on from generation to generation. As an adult, I tell the children we can undo all of this. But as an adult, I have to be straight with them. All of us have to be models in a very positive way.

Part of it is following the red road. The red road is a commitment for life. There are many exits off the red road and a lot of exits are pretty harmful. When we get off these exits, hopefully we can learn and then come back on and say, "Oh wow, I can't live that way."

Judy K. Buffalo,
Winnebago

Jennifer Siyuja of Havasupai with Cate Gilles, Flagstaff, Arizona, 1992

Sometimes the government scares me. If they keep polluting the water, the eagles might die. I also get scared when they want to put the waste dump on Prairie Island—my grandma lives there.

**Sasha Lee,
Santee Sioux,
age five**

Sasha Lee and her mother, Faye Brown, Minneapolis, Minnesota, 1992

Sasha Lee at home, Minneapolis, Minnesota, 1992

My kids are into the Indian religion because I want them to be raised not to fear but to look forward to something in life. I was determined that they would know where they came from, and what their traditions are, and to use them in their daily lives.

I try telling them, "Do not go out looking for situations; when you come to one, you will know it. Use your traditions; take time out; don't over-react. You are living in two worlds—you have got to sort both of them out." The good thing about Native American children is that if they don't make out in the white world, they always have our own world to come back to. That was the hardest thing for me—finding a link between the two.

My dream is to teach—to start my own school if I could—so students can learn about themselves and start feeling good about themselves early and not have to figure it out alone.

**Delle Big Crow,
Lakota**

Monty and William Clifford, Pine Ridge Reservation, South Dakota, 1990

Lena Dunstan and granddaughter Alicia,
Yelm, Washington, 1991

Roberta White Calf and Rocky,
Pine Ridge Reservation, South Dakota, 1992

130

I am not a very literal person, but I feel I can express myself better through my art, and that's how my students feel, too. As a teacher, I feel a need to pull the things out of them that they are afraid to say. Some of the things I am pulling out, I feel a lot of pain about, but I feel it is a good healing process. In some of my students, I see alcoholism, abuse, and even edges of suicide coming out in their artwork. But if they bring it out and they look at it, then they can deal with it better. It is all right to express your emotions, your feelings, and your pain. This is artwork for ourselves, not for the gallery downtown. It is for our own healing and healing the community.

Our communities are becoming stronger through our own self-healing process, because we have been injured and are realizing our background, where we came from, and what has caused these wounds. Now we are beginning to learn how to heal this sickness that we have been going through. I see the youth changing in their attitudes. They are taking a lot of pride in who they are and becoming more self-confident in their work.

**Jean LaMarr,
Paiute, Pit River**

Below and next page: Jean LaMarr with her students at the Institute of American Indian Arts, Santa Fe, New Mexico, 1992

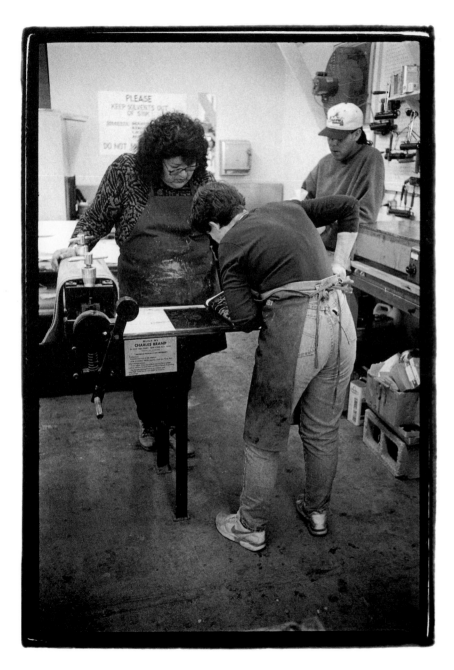

When I was in school, if you made it through eighth grade, that was it. I think when we graduated from the eighth grade, there must have been at least thirty-five students in my class, and only six of us got through high school.

I was fortunate in that I had a really supportive father and he managed to get us through high school. There were eleven of us and we all made it. Eight of us got through college, and three who didn't want to go to college went through technical school.

One of the things that we try to instill in the children here on the reservation is that they should never be ashamed to learn about their own culture, their own ceremonies. We have quite a strong group of young people who have gone back to our traditional religion. I think a good portion of it is because we were instrumental in teaching them the language and the culture. As soon as we got our own school district started, we brought the language, culture, and history in right away. We have the traditional Menominee music, which gives them a good background on the importance of the songs and the drum. This has helped the children to understand who they are, and that if they choose not to be a Catholic or a Methodist, that there's nothing wrong with them.

**Carol Dodge,
Menominee**

Carol Dodge, Menominee Reservation, Wisconsin, 1992

T., Quiltman, Char, and Brother Sun, Warm Springs, Oregon, 1992

In this day and age, we believe that our children need their education. While they are getting their education, we have to be there for them and also be speaking with them. They can see there's "say no to drugs"—they've been in those programs. You have to help them see that things are being done, so they can say "no" and mean "no." It is sad that the young people are into the drug and alcohol scene so heavily that it has ruined their lives. We still pray to the Creator that one or two will see that this lifestyle is not right. You let them know there are other things in life than their weekend parties. You do things with your children. You let them know you're happy that they are into something worthwhile. That is how you support the kids.

**Mildred Kalama Ikebe,
Nisqually, Puyallup,
Native Hawaiian**

*Jonnie Clifford with her son, Monty,
Pine Ridge Reservation, South Dakota, 1990*

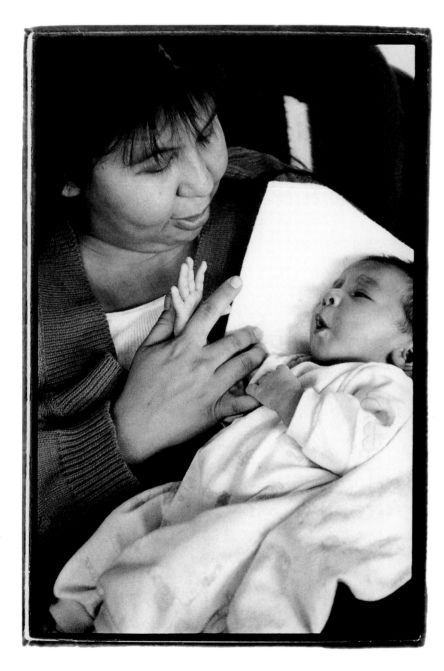

My turning point was probably when I started going to survival schools, right after I dropped out of regular school. I started hanging out at Heart of the Earth Survival School with my friend Susie.

There I saw a deerskin being tanned and attended some of the culture and language classes. That is where I started learning that there is more to our culture than just living. I went to some ceremonies, too. I was learning the hows, whys, and whats of the ceremonies and the meanings of the pipes and the eagle feathers. I was learning some of the values and why they were values to us at Heart of the Earth. And I loved it there because learning wasn't just through textbooks; it was by doing.

I work at Heart of the Earth now. I really enjoy working with the children. When I give a tour of the school, the first place I take people is to the kindergarten classroom. When we walk in, I say, "And this is our future." Working with our kids is what is important to me. Sharing the teachings that I learned at that school and passing it along is what makes me strong.

**Lisa Bellanger,
Ojibway**

Lisa Bellanger and her newborn son, Minneapolis, Minnesota, 1992

Maggie with Marilyn Pourier, Pine Ridge Reservation, South Dakota, 1990

Earth
E is for Earth
A is for Animals
R is for Respect
T is for Trees
H is for Home—what the Earth is.

Star,
Cree,
age nine

Star with Joanie Dragavon, Flagstaff, Arizona, 1986

THE WOMEN

LISA BELLANGER

(Chippewa) is a graduate of Heart of the Earth Survival School in Minneapolis, which educates children in traditional Indian ways. She grew up in the American Indian Movement and is now a mother.

PAT BELLANGER

(Chippewa) is one of the founding members of the American Indian Movement, one of the most influential Indian organizations of this century. She also cofounded Women of All Red Nations. A grandmother, she currently works with the International Indian Treaty Council.

DELLE BIG CROW

(Lakota) is the mother of five children. She grew up on the Pine Ridge Reservation in Kyle, South Dakota, during the Wounded Knee crisis and its violent aftermath. She is a teacher and traditional doll maker.

JUDY K. BUFFALO

(Winnebago) is a mother, activist, artist, and poet who lives in the Northwest.

NILAK BUTLER

(Inuit) was present during many of the violent confrontations at Pine Ridge, including a shoot-out with the FBI in 1975 and the persecution of Leonard Peltier, documented in the film *Incident at Oglala*. She is currently spearheading the efforts against nuclear weapons and nuclear-waste disposal at Greenpeace and is vice president of the Indigenous Women's Network.

DONNA CHAVIS

(Lumbee) is a mother and the Cultural Educator and Programmer at the North Carolina Cultural Center in Pembroke, North Carolina. She helped coordinate the First National People of Color's Leadership Summit, held in Washington, D.C.

KATSI COOK

(Mohawk) is the director of the Akwesasne Mother's Milk Project. She is the mother of five children, a midwife, and a writer on Native women's health.

BETTY COOPER

(Blackfeet) is a mother and is the executive director of the American Indian Family Healing Center. Using holistic approaches to treat substance abuse by Indian women, the center fosters traditional ways of healing.

CARRIE DANN

(Western Shoshone) is a rancher. She and her sister Mary have been featured in two films. One of these, *Broken Treaty at Battle Mountain,* documents their struggle to uphold Western Shoshone treaty rights. For more than twenty years, they have been defending Western Shoshone land from the avarice and greed of the Bureau of Land Management.

CAROL DODGE

(Menominee) was instrumental in starting a school district and a community college on the Menominee Reservation. She has been the acting principal at the BIA contract school on the reservation and acting director of the Native American Educational Services.

DREAMSONG

is a Lac La Ronge Band Treaty Cree from Saskatchewan, Canada.

LENA DUNSTAN

(Malkameen, Haida) is an elder and grandmother from British Columbia.

GAWANAHS (Tonya Gonnella Frichner)

(Onondaga) is the president of the American Indian Law Alliance and a member of the Native American Council of New York City. She works extensively on Native issues in the United Nations and helped to host the opening ceremonies for the Year of the Indigenous People at the UN in December of 1992.

MARY AND MELINDA GOPHER

(Ojibway) are sisters, mothers, and the founding members of Loud Thunder International, a nonprofit tax-exempt organization run by traditional Ojibway women with the goal of preserving their culture.

MILDRED KALAMA IKEBE

(Nisqually, Puyallup, Native Hawaiian) is a grandmother. Born and raised in the Northwest, she has dedicated her life to the service of others.

KANARATITAKE (Loraine Canoe)

(Mohawk) is a mother and a veteran of the Siege of Akwesasne in 1979, in which Mohawks and New York State troopers engaged in a two-year standoff. A founder of the Akwesasne Freedom School and of Women of All Red Nations, she is now a professor at Hunter College in New York City.

WINONA LaDUKE

(Mississippi Band Anishinabe) is a winner of the Reebok Human Rights Award. She is also an author, activist, and the mother of two young children. She is a founder of the Indigenous Women's Network, director of the White Earth Land Recovery Project, and serves on the board of directors of Greenpeace.

JEAN LAMARR

(Paiute, Pitt River) is an artist and printmaking professor at the Institute of American Indian Arts in Santa Fe, New Mexico.

SASHA LEE

(Santee Sioux) currently lives in Minneapolis, Minnesota.

HAZEL LITTLE HAWK

(Lakota) is a great-grandmother. She has been very active on behalf of her son, Leonard Peltier, who was imprisoned in 1975 and has become a symbol of injustice in the United States.

ARLENE LOGAN

(Seneca) is an interim Clan Mother of the Tonawanda Seneca Nation, which is a part of the six-nation Iroquois Confederacy.

LEOTA LONE DOG

(Lakota, Mohawk, Delaware) is an artist, mother, and board member of the American Indian Community House of New York City. She is also an active member of WeWah and BarCheeAmpe, the Indian gay and lesbian coalition of New York City.

SANDY JOHNSON OSAWA

(Makah) is an award-winning film producer and writer and a mother, and, with her husband, the founder of Upstream Productions in Seattle, Washington.

MAXINE PARKER

(Seneca) is a Clan Mother of the Seneca Nation in Tonawanda, New York. As with the rest of the Iroquois Confederacy, in the Seneca tribe it is the Clan Mothers who select the chiefs and hold the power to remove them.

OLIVIA POURIER

(Lakota) is a great-great-grandmother and the granddaughter of the noted Lakota spiritual leader Black Elk. She is a quilt maker and traditional doll maker and she is starting a museum in memory of her father, Ben Black Elk.

ROSEMARY RICHMOND

(Mohawk) is executive director of the American Indian Community House and is a leader of the 27,000-member New York City Indian community. She is a mother and is also a member of the Native American Council of New York City.

MARLENE RICKARD

(Tuscarora) is a grandmother. Along with her husband, Norton, she maintains traditional native plants and agricultural ways.

RENEE SENOGLES

(Red Lake Chippewa) takes a spiritual approach to her activism. She is a mother who is dedicated to the preservation of the Indian family. She teaches at Bemidji State University in Minnesota.

MYRA SOHAPPY

(Columbia River) is a longtime fishing-rights activist. Her late husband, David, and their sons were imprisoned for many years for fishing under rights granted their tribe by treaties but subsequently withdrawn. In the landmark decision *United States v. Sohappy* in 1974, the Supreme Court finally ruled that Indians were entitled to half the fish in the rivers of the Northwest.

SPIDERWOMAN THEATER,
founded by Kuna and Rappahannock sisters Lisa Mayo, Gloria Miguel, and Muriel Miguel, is among the most acclaimed Native theater groups in the country. They have created plays including *Winnetou's Snake Oil Show from Wigwam City* and, most recently, *Power Pipes*, and a short film, *Sun, Moon, and Feather*. Each of the sisters is an accomplished actress and director and has given numerous individual performances across North America.

STAR
is Lac La Ronge Band Treaty Cree from Saskatchewan, Canada.

YVONNE SWAN
(Sinixt Arrow Lakes Nation) is a mother and an advocate of prisoners' rights at the International Indian Treaty Council. In 1975, a known child molester broke into her house; in an effort to protect her children, she killed him. She was charged with murder in Washington State. The case, *Washington v. Wanrow,* (her former married name), resulted in the landmark Supreme Court decision known as the Wanrow Instruction, which expanded women's right to self-defense.

MARGO THUNDERBIRD
(Shinnecock) was an original member of the International Indian Treaty Council, and has worked to help free Native political prisoner Leonard Peltier. She was the managing editor of *Native Nations* magazine and is currently an assisting midwife and writer.

MADONNA THUNDER HAWK
(Lakota) is one of the founding members of Women of All Red Nations and was at the Wounded Knee takeover of 1973, a three-month confrontation with federal troops in South Dakota that left three Indians dead. A grandmother, she was an organizer of the Black Hills Survival Gathering in 1980.

MAE WILSON TSO
(Diné) is a grandmother and traditional sheepherder and weaver who has been fighting relocation from her home in the Mosquito Springs of Big Mountain region since 1974.

SYLVIA WALLULATUM
(Warm Springs) is an elder and grandmother who, with her sisters, has been leading a revival of the traditional ways in her community.

INGRID WASHINAWATOK-EL ISSA
(Menominee) is a longtime activist on many issues, from preventing land sales on her reservation in Wisconsin to environmental and multicultural issues in New York City. The mother of a young son, she is a member of the board of directors of the American Indian Community House and is currently working for the Fund for the Four Directions.

ROBERTA WHITE CALF
(Oglala Lakota) is a mother who worked with the Lakota tribe for seventeen years to help treat substance abuse, child abuse, and child neglect. She is currently an administrator of the Flowering Tree Project in Pine Ridge, a residential treatment center with a cultural and holistic approach for Indian women and their children.

WANBLI YAHA WIN (Karen White Eyes)
(Lakota) is a mother and professor at the Oglala Lakota College on the Pine Ridge Reservation in Kyle, South Dakota.

CHARMAINE WHITE FACE
(Oglala Lakota) is from Pine Ridge. She is a mother who used to teach math and sciences at Standing Rock Community College in North Dakota. She is currently a free-lance writer.

ESTHER YAZZIE
(Diné) is a mother of three and a Navajo interpreter for the U.S. District Courts. She was the president of the board of the Tonantzin Land Institute and co-author of the *English-Navajo Glossary of Legal Terms*. She has worked with the Cactus Valley Red Willow Springs community, who are resisting relocation. She is the founder of the Navajo Spiritual Land Recovery Project, which organizes youth leadership workshops on the reservation.

YET SI BLUE (Janet McCloud)
(Tulalip) is a great-grandmother and a longtime activist for fishing rights. She is a member of the board of directors of the Indigenous Women's Network and a founder of the Sapa Dawn Center, a nonprofit organization for Native youth empowerment.

ACKNOWLEDGMENTS

To the women who appear in the preceding pages and their families, I thank you all for your support, hospitality, and kind generosity. Alex Ewen, I thank for being my toughest critic, best friend, and companion. And I thank my parents, Rita and Jack Farley, for their unconditional support and understanding.

My deepest gratitude to my agent, Sandra Martin, and her assistant, Stephany Evans, for their belief in my work and persistence on behalf of this project, and to Holly Cara Price for introducing us in the first place and planting that formidable seed.

Thanks to Peter Ginna, Steve Topping, and Cressida Connolly of Orion Books for giving me the chance, and Peter A. Davis, art director of Orion, for his creative input. My greatest appreciation to Zoë Yanakis, Jeff Wollock, and Robbie Liben of the Solidarity Foundation for their priceless wisdom and friendship; David Levine of the Learning Alliance, who was instrumental in getting this project off the ground; Ingrid Washinawatok-El Issa for her much valued advice and direction; Heather Cook and Siena Ming Chu Tang of David Wong Custom Photo Lab; and the master printer himself, David Siu Wai Wong, for his constant support and encouragement.

A special thanks to the following individuals and organizations whose support and encouragement have made all this possible: Debbie Drake and the Professional Imaging division of the Eastman Kodak Company, Petra Ewen, Tammy Ewen, Miriam and Judith Gideon, Ellen Schneider, Brenda King, Jane Feldman, Ed Fry, Leni Sonnenfeld, and S.I.R. studios; Bobby Savene, Mell Terpos, Dan Updike, and Chuck Orozco. Special thanks to my friends at Associated Press, especially Vivian Bonati and Teri Franich. And also to Donna Daniels, Melvin Estrella, Judy Lank, and Urbano Barrera, the American Indian Community House, Rosemary

Richmond, Rudy Martin, Kent Lebsock, Jacqueline and Patrick Sheridan, Lisa and Lee Phillips, Leonard Kurz, Ruth Couch, Kerry-Jane King, Chino Bustos and Ramona Sanchez, Kalya Yannatos, Mary Richards, Fernando Natalici, Anders Goldfarb, and Sam Antiput.

Thanks to those who eased the trials and tribulations of the road: Darwin and Janet Hill and the Sah-Da-Ko-Nee Restaurant on the Tonawanda Indian Reservation; Katsi Cook and Jose Barreiro; Trudy and Roger Lauzon; the Pembletons—Sakakohe, Ray, Lisa, and Rasennes; Cecelia Square; Marlene and Norton Rickard; Faye Brown and Russ Rutter; Cherilyn Spears; Winona LaDuke; Judy Fairbanks; Bob Shimek; Delle Big Crow and Charlie Abourezk and their family; Lori Pourier and Bentley Spang; Jonnie and Billy Clifford and the boys; Marilyn, Larry, and Walt Pourier; Olivia and Hobart Pourier; Angela Anduja; Jenny DuBray and her family; Charmaine White Face and Varick Cutler; Quiltman, Charlene Napio, and T.; Anita Paz; Binah Paz; Judy Buffalo; Lee Ann LaBar; Tawna Sanchez; Mary Jane Wilson and Good Song; Carol WahPepah; Dino Butler and Juanita Whitebear; Jim Sahme; Nancy Mendoza; Agnes Mansfield; Veronica Albano; John Trudell; Esther and Bob Yazzie and family; Betty and Mae Tso; DonnaJohn; Cate Gilles; and Betty Billups; and in memory of Lisa Aguilar, Avel Escamilla, and Nancy Jean Howell.

A word of thanks to the women I missed on this last journey: Lucille Begay, Dorothy Davids, Louise Kitchkume, Betty Laverdure, Jane Martin Lone Fight, Barb Owl, and Helen Thunder.

Finally, my utmost respect and profound gratitude to the Creator for showing me the way through the creative process.

ORGANIZATIONS

✸

Here is a small listing of organizations suggested by the women in this book to contact for further information concerning Native issues:

RESEARCH AND INFORMATION

AMERICAN INDIAN LAW ALLIANCE
488 Seventh Avenue, Suite 5K
New York, NY 10018
212-268-1347

AMERICAN INDIAN MOVEMENT
2300 Cedar Avenue South
Minneapolis, MN 55407
612-724-3129

INDIAN LAW RESOURCE CENTER
601 E Street SE
Washington, DC 20003
202-547-2800

INTERNATIONAL INDIAN TREATY
COUNCIL
710 Clayton Street #1
San Francisco, CA 94117
415-566-0251

NATIVE AMERICAN COUNCIL OF
NEW YORK CITY
404 Lafayette Street
New York, NY 10003
212-765–9731

SOLIDARITY FOUNDATION
310 West 52nd Street
New York, NY 10019
212-765-9510

SOUTHWEST RESEARCH INFORMATION
CENTER
Southwest Indigenous Uranium Forum
PO Box 4524
Albuquerque, NM 87106
505-265-1862

TRADITIONAL CIRCLE OF ELDERS
AND YOUTH
PO Box 1388
Bozeman, MT 59715
406-587-1002

ISSUE-ORIENTED

ALASKA INDIGENOUS COUNCIL FOR
THE ENVIRONMENT
PO Box 1000454
Anchorage, AK 99500

APACHE SURVIVAL COALITION
PO Box 11814
Tuscon, AZ 85734
602-475-2361

COLUMBIA RIVER DEFENSE PROJECT
PO Box 184
The Dalles, OR 97058

JAMES BAY DEFENSE COALITION
310 West 52nd Street
New York, NY 10019
212-765-9731

LEONARD PELTIER DEFENSE COMMITTEE
PO Box 583
Lawrence, KS 66044
913-842-5774

NATIVE AMERICANS FOR A
CLEAN ENVIRONMENT
PO Box 1671
Tahlequah, OK 74465
918-458-4322

PRAIRIE ISLAND COALITION
PO Box 174
Lake Elmo, MN 55042
612-770-3861

WESTERN SHOSHONE DEFENSE PROJECT
General Delivery
Crescent Valley, NV 89821
702-468-0230

WEWAH AND BARCHEEAMPE
404 Lafayette Street
New York, NY 10003
212-598-0100

WHITE EARTH LAND RECOVERY PROJECT
PO Box 327
White Earth, MN 56591
218-473-3110

WOUNDED KNEE SURVIVORS
ASSOCIATION
PO Box 952
Pine Ridge, SD 57770

URBAN INDIAN CENTERS

AMERICAN INDIAN COMMUNITY HOUSE
404 Lafayette Street
New York, NY 10003
212-598-0100

MINNEAPOLIS AMERICAN INDIAN CENTER
1530 East Franklin Avenue
Minneapolis, MN 55404
612-871-4555

WOMEN-SPECIFIC

AMERICAN INDIAN FAMILY HEALING CENTER
1815 39th Avenue
Oakland, CA 94601
510-534-2737

AKWESASNE MOTHER'S MILK PROJECT
Priscilla Worswick, R.N.
Environmental Office
St. Regis Mohawk Tribe
518-358-2272

FLOWERING TREE PROJECT
Oglala Lakota Tribe
Box H
Pine Ridge, SD 57770
606-867-5904

INDIGENOUS WOMEN'S NETWORK
PO Box 174
Lake Elmo, MN 55042
612-770-3861

LOUD THUNDER INTERNATIONAL
PO Box 601
Great Falls, MT 59403

NATIVE AMERICAN WOMEN'S HEALTH
EDUCATION RESOURCE CENTER
PO Box 572
Lake Andes, SD 57356-0572

NATIVE YOUTH

AKWESASNE FREEDOM SCHOOL
c/o Akwesasne Nation
Hogansburg, NY 13683
518-358-2073

HEART OF THE EARTH SURVIVAL SCHOOL
1209 4th Street
Minneapolis, MN 55414
612-331-8862

SAPA DAWN CENTER
1013 Crystal Springs Road
Yelm, WA 98597
206-458-7610

EDUCATION

DQ UNIVERSITY
PO Box 409
Davis, CA 95617
916-758-0470

INSTITUTE OF AMERICAN INDIAN ARTS
College of Santa Fe Campus
St. Michael's Drive
Santa Fe, NM 87501-9990
505-988-6440

LEARNING ALLIANCE
494 Broadway
New York, NY 10012
212-226-7171
(tapes available from forums)

NATIVE AMERICAN EDUCATIONAL
SERVICES (NAES) COLLEGE
2838 W Peterson Avenue
Chicago, IL 60659
312-761-5000

OGLALA LAKOTA COLLEGE
PO Box 490
Kyle, SD 57752
605-455-2321

ORGANIZATION OF NORTH AMERICAN
INDIAN STUDENTS
Box 26
University Center
Northern Michigan University
Marquette, MI 49855
906-227-2138

STANDING ROCK COMMUNITY COLLEGE
HC #1 Box 4
Fort Yates, ND 58538
701-854-3861

ECONOMIC DEVELOPMENT/ SELF-SUFFICIENCY

RAMAH NAVAJO WEAVERS ASSOCIATION
PO Box 862
Ramah, NM 87321
505-775-3342

SEVENTH GENERATION FUND
PO Box 10
Forestville, CA 95436
707-887-1559

THE WEAVING PROJECT—
WOMEN IN RESISTANCE
The Survival School
1142 Guerrero Street
San Francisco, CA 94110
or
2150 47th Avenue
San Francisco, CA 94116
1-800-876-7420
415-821-9167

PERIODICALS

THE CIRCLE
Minneapolis American Indian Center
1530 East Franklin Avenue
Minneapolis, MN 55404
612-871-4555

NEWS FROM INDIAN COUNTRY
Rt. 2
Box 2900-A
Hayward, WI 54843
715-634-5226